The McQueen Foundation Beginner's Guide for Helping the Homeless

Dishambra McQueen

Beginner's Guide for Helping the Homeless

Copyright © 2018 by Dishambra McQueen.

All rights reserved.

No part of this book may be reproduced or transmitted in any form or by any means, electronic or mechanical, including photocopying, recording, or by any information storage and retrieval system, without permission in writing from the copyright author, except for the use of brief quotations in a book review.

Published in the United States by
Pen2Pad Ink Publishing.

Requests to publish work from this book or to contact the author should be sent to:
contact@mcqueenfoundation.com

Dishambra McQueen retains the rights
to all images

Interior design: Pen2Pad Ink Publishing

Beginner's Guide for Helping the Homeless

This Book is dedicated to :

Joyce Ruth McQueen (GrandGrand)

To The McQueen Foundation... Every moment of every day of my life you are with me! You inspire me to keep going, you continuously remind me that there is always a new level to reach and together we will explore them all. Each of you are a gift from God and not a day goes by where I am not thankful for your existence, your time, your support, and the love you've shown me over the last 3 years.

To Arketa Williams and Ginette Lewis... Thank You for your extraordinary support in this process. I was in a very discouraging place in my life when this book was written. I went to both of you and said, "I'm done!" Knowing how it feels to have your back against the wall, neither of you allowed me to live in that moment. Each of you reminded me that troubles don't last always. The only thing that comes from pain is growth. Then you encouraged me to take on one of my biggest fears at the time which was writing. Growing up with dyslexia, writing was the last thing I wanted to do but because of your encouragement I found another way to help others. I sincerely thank you.

Table of Contents

1. Business vs. Pleasure... 11
2. Developing Your Organization........................... 15
3. Gaining Experience... 21
4. Marketing Your Organization........................... 25
5. Establishing Credibility....................................... 31
6. Budgeting and Fundraising................................ 35
7. Getting Volunteers.. 45
8. Logistics.. 53
9. Building Rapport With the
   Homeless Community... 63
10. Quick Tip Guide... 69
11. About the Author... 73
12. Resources.. 75
13. Glossary.. 83

Beginner's Guide for Helping the Homeless

Homelessness is defined as the circumstance when people don't have a permanent place to live such as a house or apartment. For many homeless individuals, this wasn't a choice they made - it was a series of events that caused the outcome. They simply fell on hard times and weren't able to recover. Since 2016 over 15 million homes have been foreclosed on. For others, they were simply unable to acquire and maintain regular, safe, secure and adequate housing.

In the United States there are over 600,000 homeless people on any given night, many of which are sleeping in either in homeless shelters or some kind of short-term housing. More than a third are living in cars, under bridges, or are in some other way living unsheltered. One in five homeless people suffers from untreated severe mental illness.

Did you know that...

- More than 90 percent of homeless women are victims of severe physical or sexual abuse?

- Over 138,000 of the homeless in the U.S. are children under the age of 18. Thousands of these homeless children are unaccompanied. In 2017, local schools districts reported there were over 1 million homeless children in public schools.

- Over 57,000 veterans are homeless each night. Of that, sixty percent of them are in shelters while the rest are unsheltered. Nearly 5,000 of these veterans are women.

- Males make up 85 percent of the homeless population.

Our goal as an organization is to change the lives of as many of the homeless as possible by providing them with basic necessities, words of prayer, wisdom, and encouragement, as well as knowledge and information about places that can help them change their situation. We are very hands-on in our efforts as it strives to fight hunger, homelessness, and poverty.

For those who share this same passion, this book is designed to be a tool to assist you with helping the 600,000 homeless people in need of assistance. If you are trying to develop an organization or business, get volunteers, and expand your reach - this book will aid you in your process. We wish you much success on your journey!

"If You Think You Can Change The World YOU CAN!"

- McQueen Foundation

Business vs. Pleasure

I can't stress to you enough the importance of your image. Your image can make or break your business which is why separating your business from your personal life is extremely important.

Creating a business page doesn't mean people aren't going to look at your personal page. Not only will they look, they will judge you based off of what they see. Once you begin regularly volunteering, developing a business and shining a light on the work you do with other people - you are also shining a light on yourself. Here are some tips on how to maintain a business and publicly acceptable persona, even on the personal side of your "social media life:"

- Find new outlets to "vent." Reach out to trusted friends, your church family, learn (or increase) meditation, etc. The main thing is to find ways to vent OFFLINE.

- Always remember when you are out there are people watching you – and how you treat others.

- Remember that your organization should be available and welcoming of ALL who need the assistance you provide. Regardless of how you feel about certain "hot topics" in society, NO social media posts should exclude or discriminate against anyone based on sexual orientation, politics, religion, ethnicity, etc. While you may be very passionate about some of these topics, it's best to leave them off social media.

You never want someone to feel as if they can't be around you unless they conform to your beliefs. This will reflect badly on your organization and people won't want to be around you. This will result in you having difficulty finding people and other organizations to support what you're doing.

At the end of the day, when people locate you on social media they should be able to see your organization through you. You are the face and brand of your business, and this is especially true when you're new. It's important to be aware of your actions and image at all times.

Quick Tips

- REPRESENT! You are a representation of your brand at all times.

- BE A LEADER! Lead by example.

- BE CAREFUL! First impressions are lasting impressions and negative impressions spread quickly and last a long time.

Beginner's Guide for Helping the Homeless

"There is no exercise better for the heart than reaching down and lifting people up."

-John Holmes

Developing Your Organization

Now that you've made up in your mind that you're going to develop an organization to serve the homeless, begin developing it. Use the following tips to get started:

- Establish your "why?" Write down why you want to connect with the homeless in your community. What do you want to accomplish?

- What will you do? What services do you offer? What do these services consist of?

- Determine the needs of the homeless that you want your organization to focus on. For instance, do you want to focus on their needs (housing, clothing, food, mental health, health care), or a particular demographic in the homeless population (men, women, children, etc.).

- Begin creating the mission, core values, and objectives you desire for your organization

- Begin the process of creating a name for your organization. You will find that this is much harder than you expect. More than being "catchy," make sure your name has a story and meaning behind it.

- Create a letterhead with your company's name and contact information on it.

- What will you use for your company's contact information? Are you going to purchase a phone and get a new number strictly for your business, set up a Google voice phone number that will send the messages to your cell phone, or are you going to use your current cell phone as your business phone as well?

- What is the organization's email address?

- If someone wanted to mail in donations to your organization are you going to give them your home address or will you set up a P.O. Box for your organization?

- Will your organization need a website? If so, do you have an idea of what you want to use for a domain name? Is it available?

- Create a budget for your organization. Be sure to cover the following in your budget:
    - Marketing
    - Event space
    - Activities
    - Expenses

Once you've developed a written concept of your organization, register your organization with the IRS. You do this by obtaining a tax id number or EIN. An EIN is An Employer Identification Number (EIN) is used to identify a business entity. Generally, businesses need an EIN. To complete the process go to https://www.irs.gov/businesses/small-businesses-self-employed/employer-id-numbers and complete the form. It doesn't cost to request it and you obtain the number instantly.

When you get your organization is developed you will want to file it as a nonprofit (501(c)3) so you can get funding and donations for your organization. You'll need the EIN in order to complete the 1023 form to register your organization as a nonprofit. There is a short version of this form called the 1023EZ form. I recommend you go to
https://www.irs.gov/forms-pubs/about-form-1023ez and start with the 1023EZ form.

There are a series of questions you'll have to answer to determine which form you have to complete and how much you will need to pay. The user fee for Form 1023 is $600. The user fee for Form 1023-EZ is $275, The Form 1023-EZ fee must be paid through www.pay.gov when the application is filed. Payments can be made directly from your bank account or by credit/debit card so have the information ready when you sit down to start your paperwork.

Developing your organization can be a very exciting –

and very stressful - experience. Keep it simple and always remind yourself of the end goal - running a quality organization that is effectively in helping the homeless population in your community.

You have to be the leader and the provider for your organization so your volunteers can feel they are putting their time into something meaningful and productive. Stick to the purpose and the mission of the organization at all times, no matter how big your organization gets. Prepare a small introduction about your organization so that any time someone asks you "What does your organization do?" You won't stumble.

Quick Tips

- EVALUATE YOU! Always be able to identify your organization strengths and weaknesses.

- PLAN AHEAD! Your organization needs comprehensive planning just has much as a business does.

- STRIVE TO GROW! Always develop goals for your organization.

"You have not lived today until you have done something for someone who can never repay you."

- John Bunyan

Gaining Experience

Before beginning to host your own events and establishing programs for your organization to work with the homeless, I recommend you connect with other organizations who are already working with them first.

While you may not understand why until much later, it's important that you begin to develop a habit now of giving back to other organizations. One of the biggest advantages of doing this is *gaining experience* – not judging the organization, but learning from it.

While volunteering, you should also be doing an assessment to see what they do, how you can do it, and what areas you can improve upon within your own organization.

First, start with assessing how the organization treats you; ask yourself the following:

- Did you feel appreciated?
- Were you acknowledged?

- Did you ask all your desired questions?
- Were all your questions answered?
- What is the atmosphere like?
- How did the organization treat the homeless?
- Were they friendly and upbeat or down right mean

It is very true: you can always tell the character of a person or an organization by the way they treat the people they say they're helping.

In addition to assessing the organization as you volunteer with them, this is also a good time to do a self-evaluation of whether starting an organization to help the homeless is the right decision for you. Take some time to ask yourself the following questions after your first few interactions as a volunteer:

- How did you feel being there?
- Is this something you can do long term?
- What was your comfort level around the homeless population?
- Can you commit to serving the homeless regardless of the weather? They need assistance the most during times of extreme heat and cold – have you volunteered during those times?

Here is the bottom line: BE the volunteer that you want to volunteer for you. Lead by example! Everybody is looking at you and they will remember if you're the one that helped – or hindered – their progress.

Quick Tips

- GIVE OF YOURSELF! Use your personal skill or talent to assist the homeless.

- EDUCATION! Educate others about homelessness.

- BE EMPATHETIC! Seek to understand people who are homeless.

"You can never go wrong by investing in communities and the human beings within them."

–Pam Moore, CEO of Marketing Nutz

Marketing Your Organization

Start marketing your organization by creating your brand. When you begin creating your brand you want to think about how you want people to view your organization. What do you represent? What do you stand for? When you are branding yourself, people are seeing a representation of you before they ever physically lay eyes on you. So what type of impression are you making?

How you brand yourself will determine the growth of your organization. There are good ways to start branding yourself.

- **Logo**
    - Make sure your logo connects with what you're doing. Don't pick a logo of your face it's not about you and don't pick a logo of something that has nothing to do with your business.

- **Slogan**
    - Your slogan should be something that

catches people attention and draws them in to want to know more.

- **Website**
    - You want to provide the same information on your website that you would if you were talking directly to an individual face to face.

- **Marketing Plan**
    - Create a strategic plan for marketing your organization. How are you going to get the word out and tell people you exist?
    - Are you only going to post on social media?
    - Are you going to create flyers and hand them out door to door?
    - Are you volunteer with organizations and spreading the word about your organization?
    - Are you going to sponsor other events under your company's name?
    - Is your organization going to partner with other organizations to put on an event for the homeless?
    - What are you going to do? What is your plan of action?

- **Inexpensive Marketing Strategies**
    - Canva www.canva.com is a great website with quick and easy to-use templates for all social media platforms. This takes the guesswork out of designing images for social media and allows you to create more quality graphics.

- Pablo https://pablo.buffer.com creates beautiful images that will make your social media campaign pop.

- Have t-shirts, cups, towels, pens, etc. with your company's name and contact information on it that can be passed out to businesses and volunteers.

- Shindiz.com and Orientaltrading.com are both good websites for getting personalized items. They also offer a variety of different discounts throughout the year.

From the moment you first begin marketing your organization your marketing needs to remain consistent. Especially when marketing on social media. You cannot gain a following or develop a presence on social media posting once every other six months. Your lack of consistency will reflect negatively on your organization before you can even get it running good. No one will want to work with an inconsistent organization.

When establishing your presence on social media the follow it's very important to do the following:

- Connect and engage with your volunteers.
- Connect and engage with people who are interested in what you're doing - they can become potential volunteers.
- Respond to their inbox messages.
- Respond back to any comments they enter

below your content.
- Show your appreciation when they praise you for doing something.
- Pour back into your volunteers on a level that can help them in their personal life by posting inspiration and encouraging messages.

As you give back to others it will in turn be given to you.

Quick Tips

- INVEST! Invest in yourself.

- BE CONSISTENT! Respond to people in a timely Manner.

- STAY IN TOUCH! Connect and engage with others.

Beginner's Guide for Helping the Homeless

"There is nothing more beautiful than someone who goes out of their way to make life beautiful for others."

- Mandy Hale

Establishing Credibility

Establishing credibility is a key metric in the success of your organization. To gain donors, sponsors, volunteers, or even the trust of those in the homeless community, you and your organization must be seen as trustworthy, secure, competent, and solid. Here are a few small tips you can use to get started:

- Trust your volunteers and earn their trust by showing them you know what you're doing, and where the organization is heading.

- Always keep your word, meet deadlines, and be clear about what you want.

- Be the leader! Honor the mission and values of your organization at all times and serve as the best example of how to represent them.

- Keep the needs of the homeless community you're serving as the primary focus.

- Be accountable. Acknowledge when you have made mistakes and work quickly to correct them.

- Give the respect you want given to you.

- Always have a plan for the next level of growth for the organization. Never get stagnant or complacent.

In addition to volunteering for other organizations, partnering with them is a plus for you in many more ways than one. By partnering you are creating a bigger support system that can serve more homeless people! Partnering means more donations, more resources, and ultimately, more assistance being available for your homeless community.

Additionally, you increase your pool of volunteers. Though your current volunteers may love what they do, the reality is they could become burned out if they don't take proper time to rest, and their respective life situations could change, altering their ability to continue to volunteer for you. A bigger volunteer base provides you with the ability to have longer rotations among volunteers, and more opportunity to be in more places to help more people.

Below of a list of organizations, you can start with when looking into partnering with.

- Local Organizations

- Local Homeless Shelters
- Bike Clubs
- Social Clubs
- Wal-Mart
- Exxon Mobil
- Goodwill
- Churches
- Community Centers

Be sure to give! Give before you receive. The more we give, the happier we feel. Giving increases self-confidence. You are doing good for others and the community which provides a sense of accomplishment. Once you become a giver you will never go without therefore you don't look into receiving things all the time. The more you put into your organization the more you can ask for when things are needed. Once volunteers see that you are producing more than what you're asking for they will be willing to give you more

Quick Tips

- DARE TO BELIEVE! Believe in your cause. If you don't believe in what you're doing you'll have a hard time getting others to believe in you.

- TIME! Your time means more than everything.

- LEAD! Remember you are a leader at all times. Leading by example is of the utmost importance.

"Every cent you own and every moment you spend is always an investment."

- Natalie Pace

Budgeting and Fundraising

Regardless of your comfort level with "asking for money," your organization CANNOT get off the ground without funds. Fundraising is one of the most important areas of developing your organization and it will be very important for you to take the time to learn the jargon, and the options available to you for funding assistance at the local, regional, and national level.

Whether you're asking for donations face-to-face or via social media, it's important to make sure those you're seeking donations from have the following questions answered up front:

- What does your organization do and why should they care?
- What are the goals you have for the organization?
- What needs do you have for the organization?
- How will their donation help you accomplish the goals or meet the needs you have?

As you get those questions answered you now want to begin focusing on the best way to approach donors:

- Research your donor as an individual: Do they give often? How do they currently interact with your organization, if at all?

- Never surprise your prospect. Make it clear in your first interaction that you're interested in talking to them about your cause and how they might be able to get involved.

- Think about what can be offered in return – whether it be a plaque, ad space, a prominent place on marketing materials...get creative!

- Understand that there will be "No's." Understanding this now, will help you to not get discouraged when it happens.

- Make them understand why you need what you are asking for. Be clear, without sounding needy or desperate. Be passionate, without being too aggressive.

Now, it's time to start asking:

- Create eye-catching punch lines
- Don't wait to ask
- Explain and describe what you want to do
- Keep it personal

- Provide links and ways to give
- Follow up and say thank you
- Keep it short and sweet
- Have confidence
- Show your previous work
- Make non-monetary ask

If you are requesting donations via social media or other communication mediums, it is strongly suggested you develop an on-the-spot "ad" answering the above questions in less than 30 seconds (if audio) or no more than 256 characters (if written)...this will allow you to be clear about the needs in a way that keeps the attention of your audience and potential donors. If you are requesting donations face-to-face, this same ad will help you get to the point AND sound much more confident and professional. Finally, a donation letter should be crafted and readily available as you begin to reach out for donations via mail, email, and when visiting businesses door-to-door.

Getting donations from businesses as a 501(c)3

If you haven't already started the process of obtaining a 501(c)3 nonprofit status through the IRS, you should begin that immediately. While you don't need to be a nonprofit to serve the homeless community, there are several benefits to having that designation:

- Those who donate to you will be able to write the donations off on their taxes at the end of

- the year; thus giving THEM potential tax savings while helping YOU reach your goals.

- You will be eligible for government grants and other assistance that is only available to those who have the nonprofit designation.

- As your organization grows, you will be able to enjoy tax-exempt purchases for items you need, in addition to exemption from federal, state, local, and in some case, payroll taxes. All of this adds up to huge savings over time.

- An official 501(c)3 designation makes your organization more "official," and "legitimate," which will assist you in future fundraising efforts.

There are numerous companies across the country that donate gift cards, in-kind donations, or other items to non-profits. There are too many to list; however, here are a few companies and the links to apply for donations.

- The Container Store (Arizona and Texas locations only)
http://standfor.containerstore.com/our-commitment-to-our-communities/

- Jason's Deli

https://www.jasonsdeli.com/donation-requests

- Sprouts

    https://about.sprouts.com/culture-and-community/

- Total Wine & More
  https://www.totalwine.com/about-us/donation-requests

- Fogo De Chao (Arizona and Texas locations only) https://fogodechao.com/donation/

- Food Conspiracy Co-op

    http://www.foodconspiracy.coop/donation-requests/online-donation-request/

- Dallas Cowboys
  https://dallascowboys.requestitem.com/

- Dallas Mavericks
  https://www.mavs.com/community/donation-requests/

- Dallas Stars
  https://www.nhl.com/stars/community/

- Dallas Zoo
  https://www.dallaszoo.com/about-us/charitable-donation-requests/

- Jumpstreet Indoor Trampoline Park
  https://www.gotjump.com/donations/

- Six Flags Over Texas (Arlington, TX)
  https://www.sixflags.com/overtexas/community/ticket-donations

- SeaWorld San Antonio
  https://seaworldsanantonio.wufoo.com/forms/z1yz65k00xvqzyp/

- Topgolf (Arizona, Oklahoma, and Texas locations)
  https://topgolf.com/us/company/giving/donation-criteria/

- Waste Management
  http://www.wm.com/about/community/charitable-giving.jsp

- Whataburger
  https://whataburger.com/community/applyforsupport

- Whole Foods
  https://www.wholefoodsmarket.com/donate

- Walmart
  http://giving.walmart.com/apply-for-grants/

What Businesses Donate to Nonprofits?

There are millions of businesses that donate to an organization, but in 2017 these companies donated a total of **$3.5 billion in cash**:

- Gilead Sciences
- Wal-Mart
- Wells Fargo
- Goldman Sachs Group
- Chevron
- JPMorgan Chase
- Alphabet (Google)
- Citigroup

It's very important that you do your research when reaching out to a business. Look at their history in funding organizations. Feel free to look more into the companies that are listed.

Keeping track of your donations

It is a MUST that you keep accurate records of your donations, along with providing receipts to those who donate to you to keep for their records. While the 501(c)3 designation from the IRS will assist you greatly in your efforts to fund your organization, it will always be in your best interest to always document the donations, along with how the money has been used, in case you are ever asked for an account of how you're spending the money you receive. The last thing you want is to be audited.

While accepting donations be sure to get a receipt book to keep track of cash donations. Receipt books can be purchased at Walmart for between $3-5.00.

Applying for grants

Another way to get funding for your nonprofit is by applying for grants. Applying for grants is a very time consuming process so generate a grant proposal before you begin. You'll need it when completing the applications. When applying be sure to take your time and carefully read the instructions.

Listed below are a few that organizations servicing hunger issues and homelessness can visit to apply for grants.

- Grants.gov

- Substance Abuse and Mental Health Service Administration (SAMHSA) https://www.samhsa.gov/homelessness-programs-resources/grant-programs-services

- Family & Youth Service Bureau (FYSB) https://www.acf.hhs.gov/fysb/grants

- Administration for Children and Families https://ami.grantsolutions.gov/index.cfm?switch=searchresult&type=office&param=ACYF_FYSB&page=ACYF%20/%20FYSB

- Windermere Foundation
  https://www.windermere.com/foundation
  (scroll all the way to the bottom of the page for the application)

- Oak Foundation
  http://www.oakfnd.org/housing-and-homelessness.html or
  http://www.oakfnd.org/grant-database-hh.html

- Safeway Foundation
  http://safewayfoundation.org/get-funded/grant-funding-guidelines-jewel-osco/

- H.J. Heinz Company Foundation
  https://www.tgci.com/funding-sources/funders/hj-heinz-company-foundation

- ConAgra Foods Foundation
  http://www.conagrabrands.com/our-company/conagra-brands-foundation

- Food Lion Charitable Foundation
  https://www.foodlion.com/in-our-community/food-lion-feeds/charitable-foundation-grants/

- Albertson's Community Relations
  http://national.albertsonscompaniesfoundation.org/get-funded/

Beginner's Guide for Helping the Homeless

Quick Tips

- **RECYCLE!** Stay within budget by being aware of all the donated items. Some of items may be able to be washed out and reused at multiple events.

- **SHOW GRATITUDE!** Don't forget to say thank you!

- **BE FRIENDLY!** It costs you nothing to be kind to someone else.

"You make a living by what you get. You make a life by what you give."

- Winston Churchill

Getting Volunteers

Oftentimes, getting volunteers is as simple as looking right under your nose. Many people starting organization find that their friends and family are more than willing to help them get started. If you find however, that you don't have the support of your circle, or have grown and need additional support, here are some things you can do:

- Ask your friends and family if they or someone they know might want to volunteer.

- Ask the volunteers you currently have for volunteer referrals. A recommendation from a friend is worth much more than one from someone you don't know. Also, if every volunteer asks a friend who asks another friend, you will reach your goal faster than you could imagine

- Post about your need on various volunteer websites and on social media. Give people the opportunity say decide if they want to be an volunteer

- Go to your local city hall and register your organization with the state. This allows those with community service obligations due to tickets, etc. to conduct their community service with your organization.

Respecting your support - How to treat volunteers

The saying "treat others the way you want to be treated," applies to volunteers as well:

- Respect their time – Volunteers have other lives and obligations like you do. If you're unable to keep an appointment, notify the volunteer as soon as possible. When events are created, give them enough notice so they are able to make arrangements to assist. If you have to cancel an event, the volunteers need to be the first to know.

- Make it easy for them to volunteer. Don't ask for unrealistic donations or favors. Also make sure you're not giving them "grunt work," or tasks you just don't want to do yourself. Volunteers who feel used, won't volunteer very long.

- Don't down talk to any race, religion or sexually orientation. Volunteers come in all shapes, sizes, colors and genders - the last thing you want to do is offend someone who's helping you.

- If you are unaware of a volunteer's name address them as Ma'am or Sir and then make the effort to find and remember their name.

Re-paying your volunteers

There are multiple ways to show your volunteers you appreciate them, and what they do:

- o Celebrate recognition days like **International Volunteer Day** and **National Volunteer week**.
- o Give out awards certificates with your volunteers' name on it to show them appreciation.
- o Take individual pictures of your volunteers at various events. Print them out with the words "'Thank you" on the back of the picture.
- o Provide food for the volunteers at your events.
- o Tell them when they have done a great job.
- o Get to know your volunteers. Be an additional source of assistance or support should they find themselves going through a tough time.
- o Say "Thank you" often.

Developing leaders - How to mentor your volunteers

The goal in mentoring your volunteers should be to pour all the knowledge you have about the homeless into them. You want them to be able to go out into the homeless community without you in confidence. Some volunteers serve with organizations because they feel they don't know what to do, or are afraid. If you continue to support and encourage them

they will feel more confident in serving the community without supervision. You want to be able to give them necessary independence, strength, and personal accountability for them to lead others. Allow them to

lead before they are a leader. Equip them with resources and coaching. Give them small tasks at each event that you would usually take care of. There is no better training than hands-on training! Once you assign a volunteer to a new role, allow them to grow in other areas as well.

Note: All volunteers do not want to lead. That's normal and ok!

Accepting voluntary requests to be a vendor for your event

When you allow vendors to set up at your event make sure you conduct a background check on them to ensure they are qualified. Check their social media pages. Look at pictures of previous work they have done. Find out if they are licensed or not.

If they are a barber attending your event for the sole purpose of providing haircuts for the men ask the following questions:

- Do they have electric clippers?
- Do they have a way to clean the clippers?
- How do they intend to clean up behind

- themselves?
- Will they be bringing their own cleaning supplies to clean their area?
- Will a table be needed or will they be bringing their own?
- Are they going to stay for the duration of the event or will they only be there for a portion of it?
- How many heads can they cut at one time?

If they can only cut 30 heads but you have 100 people needing haircuts create a separate section just for them. Then have everyone ready to go upon arrival.

If they are a hairstylist attending your event to provide hairstyles ~~to~~ for the women ask the following questions:

- Will they need water?
- How will they clean the brushes and combs?
- How are they being sanitized?
- Do they have the proper materials to make sure their tools are sanitized after each individual?
- What type of hair styles are they going to do?

All the hairstyles need to be basic and simple. Braids or style cuts only. You don't want to spend the entire event doing one person's hair. DO NOT allow the stylist to use chemicals or heat. You don't want to be responsible for any incidents.

If you plan on bringing in a DJ for your event research their history. Go to their next upcoming event to listen to their style and see how they connect with the audience. Make sure they cater to the crowd that's being serviced. Make sure they play happy music. Know your audience and make sure they can adapt to it. The goal is to make them forget about
their current situation. If hiring a DJ isn't in your budget and you decide to simply play music from your phone that is perfectly ok too. Just make sure your music is connecting with your audience.

Quick Tips

- **BE COURTEOUS!** Respond with kindness

- **KEEP IN TOUCH!** Never lose touch with your volunteer be relatable

- CLEAN UP!!! When you complete an event make sure you thoroughly clean up behind yourself.

"You may not have saved a lot of money in your life, but if you have saved a lot of heartaches for other folks, you are a pretty rich man."

- Seth Parker

Logistics

Don't wait until the last minute to start preparing for your event. Create a checklist for your event weeks before its scheduled date. I recommend that you start by adding the main items for your event. Main items are those items you cannot go without. Items such as tables and chairs.

Tables are something that you should always bring with you. Without tables there is no place for your volunteers to setup food or donations. Should you desire to purchase your own tables this is an example of a 6" folding table that can be purchased at your local Walmart for approximately $39.00. Prices may vary according to the different location.

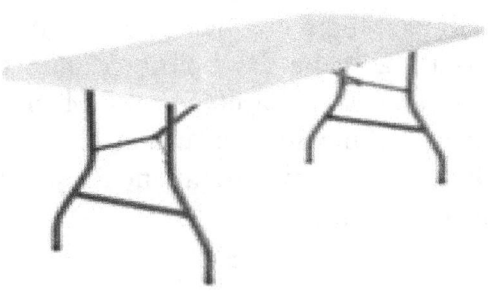

Beginner's Guide for Helping the Homeless

Chairs are another main item that you should bring. I would suggest you have at least two. The chairs should primarily be for the homeless or a volunteer that is unable to stand. Should you desire to purchase your chairs this standard mainstream steel folding chair can be purchased at your local Walmart for approximately $9.83. Prices may vary according to the different location.

Know the best days and times to host a homeless event.

For the homeless community there is never a good or bad time to serve them. However, I've learned the best days to feed them are the day before or after the 1st of the month, and the day before or after the 15th of the month. This is primarily because of the volunteers. These days coincide with when they tend to get assistance from the government and are more willing to contribute donations.

When it comes to picking a date, set it for the weekend verses the weekday. Volunteers tend to have more flexibility with their schedules on the weekends than they do during the week.

Once you've selected a date the next thing you need to do is choose a time. You want to have your events early in the mornings so you don't interfere with any activities volunteers may have planned with their families. Luckily the homeless community is very rarely crowded so I recommend feeding and serving them when it's in your heart to do so. They will always appreciate it.

Picking a good location for your event.

Now it's time to pick a location. Any location where the homeless lives is a good location. However, when you are trying to pick a location for public events there are a few things to consider:

- Is there location close by that provides a restroom, specifically for children and the elderly?

- Are there covered shelters to block sun or rain? Even if the spot you're serving at doesn't have shelter try to pick a spot that is close to shelter just in case.

- Pick a location that's not around a lot of traffic. At these events you will have people walking everywhere from volunteers to the homeless.

- It's your responsibility to make sure everyone is safe and away from moving cars.

- Do NOT set up in front of a business without permission from the business owner (NOT the manager). It is your duty to respect everyone and that includes businesses that may be nearby.

- Bringing the appropriate items for hygiene and sanitary use is very important. Here are the TOP items to bring to a homeless outreach event:
    - Soap or no-rinse body soap
    - No rinse shampoo
    - Toothpaste/Toothbrushes
    - Bug spray
    - Deodorant
    - Baby Wipes
    - Toilet paper
    - Medicated Body powder
    - Small trash bags
    - Feminine products
    - Diapers
    - Manicure set (Nail clippers, Nail Brush)
    - Hand Sanitizer

Setting up food tables for the homeless outreach event

When setting up the food tables at your event here are a few things you will always need to be present on the table:

- Table cloths
- Serving gloves
- Tash bags
- Hand sanitizer
- Serving utensils
- Foil paper
- Plasticware and napkins
- Food
- Plastic containers with lids
- Silver plastic pans

When you are placing the items on the table it needs to be set up as an assembly line. The better you organize your table, the easier it will be to serve mass amount of individuals. Follow the example below when you are serving sandwiches. For all other meal plans adjust yourself accordingly.

- Hand sanitizer should be first. This allows the homeless to clean their hands before they eat and also allow the volunteers to clean their hands before they serve.
- The gloves will go next for the volunteers to place on their hands immediately after applying sanitizer.
- To-go containers
- Bread
- Mustard, mayo etc.
- Meats

- Sides (lettuce, tomatoes, onions etc.)
- Chips
- Plasticware
- Drinks

You want to prepare the meal in order.

Setting up clothes closets or tables

When setting up a clothing table you should separate the items by gender and by size. This will make the process easier and faster. When someone approaches the table ask them their gender. Do not assume. Next, ask what size they wear. Depending on how many people you have you'll need to make a judgement on how many items you can give them but the goal is to never take anything home!

Establishing control during the event with no help

Sometimes your event can consist of just you. In those instances organization is key to maintaining control as you attempt to help others. I know some of you are thinking there's no way you can do an entire event alone but believe it or not it is very possible as long as you are prepared, have everything organized, operate within one area so that everything you need is easily accessible, and remain calm and in control of your work station.

Placing your volunteers at your event

When you're going to have an event with volunteers, start by preparing weeks before the event. It's good to keep a notebook or notepad with all of your notes so they are in one place. Know what items go where and how many people you will need at each table. Once the volunteers arrive, go over their positions with them. Once you give each volunteer their position have them go to their respective locations.

When everyone is in place take a moment to evaluate the whole set up. Look for any areas that may need more help so when the remaining volunteers arrive you can already know where they should be stationed. You should be on your feet at all times, and aware of everything going on. When things are out of place, fix it immediately. Regardless of how many people are asking for your help, stay calm and remember you can only help one person at a time. The KEY is being organized and prepared.

Creating Care Packages

You may decide to provide care packages to those in the homeless community to take with them at the end of your outreach event. Below is a list of non-perishable items you can use:

- Granola bars
- Fruit snacks

Beginner's Guide for Helping the Homeless

- Applesauce
- Crackers with peanut butter or cheese
- Water bottle
- Socks
- Hand wipes
- Lifesavers or sugar free gum
- Deodorant
- Hand lotion
- Dental Floss
- Positive Book
- Chapstick

Quick Tips

- NEVER EVER Let Anyone Beat You to Your Event!!!

- BE PREPARED! Enter every event as if you're the only one who's going to be there. The event MUST go on.

- SAFETY! Be aware of your surroundings at all times. You are responsible for the safety of both the homeless and your volunteers.

"Good works is giving to the poor and the helpless, but divine works is showing them their worth to the One who matters."

- Criss Jami

Building Rapport With The Homeless Community

Taking on a personal approach is the number one way to build a relationship with the homeless. You want them to feel that you as a person really care and they are not just another number or business to you. Sympathize with them. Listen to them. Hug them. Show humanity.

Feed the homeless on your own time. This will show them that you are not just coming around when there's a crowd. This gives you the chance to build one-on-one relationships and possible friendships. You're able to learn more about them, and possibly discover more ways to help.

Being with the homeless alone gives some of them a sense of security and makes them open up more to you. This is your opportunity to ask questions and find out the things that they enjoy. It could even be their favorite music. When planning your next event, you can use all the new ideas you've received and make it even better.

How to talk to the homeless:

- It's important that you have a positive attitude and be in good spirits If you are having personal problems please put them aside.

- Start a normal conversation. You don't have to go into a long conversation but a small conversation may brighten their day and yours. Ask them where they are from or if they have children. It's ok to ask them their story but be prepared if they don't want to share details with you.

- Be respectful and create boundaries.
  Remember everyone is human and entitled to his or her human rights. Some questions aren't meant to be asked.

- Don't do all the talking; let them talk to you. Your goal is to understand those you're serving, not the other way around.

- Don't feel pressured to offer money. It's ok to say *"I don't have any money, but is there another way I can help you?"* Sometimes the non-monetary things last longer.

- Always think first about your safety first. Never offer rides in your car to someone you don't know and never stand with anyone in a poorly lit place. If you feel unsafe don't worry

   about being rude. Just leave the situation. Your safety is a top priority, always.

Mapping homeless community areas, zones.

Familiarize yourself with the homeless resources in your area so that when you're speaking with the homeless you can direct them to the nearest shelter or soup kitchen. They may be passing through town and be unaware that there is a resource close by. An example: *"How are you doing? There's a soup kitchen over on Jefferson Street, and I think they're open for dinner around five. You should check it out."*

Your organization may not be able to assist in all areas so you want to find a place near the homeless community that they can go to for assistance. Introduce yourself to other outreach resources so they can be familiar with you.

Assessing the needs of the community

The most effective way to know the needs of the homeless community is by asking them. Below are ways to break down who needs what:

- Age Breakdown
- Gender

- Sexual Orientation
- Race/Ethnicity
- Employment status
- Educational Status

Once you've collected the above information you can group them according to their needs. When doing assessments, sometimes it's good to simply sit back and observe things. Sitting in a car close by monitoring the activities of the homeless will give you a chance to see the bigger needs.

How to handle mean and angry people:

When dealing with people not everyone is friendly.

- **Be aware -** As with any other group of people, not all poor people will repay your kindness and understanding. Some are drug addicts, career criminals, dossers and economic migrants.

- **Be forgiving -** If someone doesn't respond warmly to your efforts don't hold it against them. Not everyone will respond – they might have had a bad day or had someone be not so nice to them around the corner Simply say, " I'm sorry, I didn't mean to offend you."

How to know if a homeless person is deceiving you

- Food: Anyone that's truly down on their luck will gladly take any food that is offered to them, even if they just ate.

- Surroundings: If a person is running a scam, they could be part of a larger group. They may have a car parked close by for a getaway. Look for any abandoned cars.

- Pay attention to the way they interact with you: Are they rushing you to give them money? Looking over their shoulder or yours a lot? Are they giving you eye contact, or purposely looking away?

- Shoes say a lot (Donated or not): Do they look relatively recent and new? How worn are they?

When all said and done, be wise and trust your gut.

Picture and image etiquette

Try to take pictures at your event without including the homeless. How would you like to have some strangers walk into your house and start taking pictures of all your personal belongings? Or for some strangers to just start getting in your face with cameras?

Well, that's how you should look at the homeless' desire for privacy. You are in their personal space and it's very rude to disrupt their privacy without asking.

When you are hosting a homeless outreach event, please refrain from taking pictures of the homeless.

There are ways around taking pictures of the event and your volunteers without including the homeless. If a homeless individual person asks to take

pictures, that is perfectly fine. This all goes back to respect others space and treating them the way you want to be treated.

Quick Tip Guide

In this guide you will discover additional quick and easy tips that can aid you in your developmental process.

- **STICK TO YOUR PLAN!** Don't change the flow of things at the last minute. You don't want to appear to be all over the place.

- **HAVE SUPPORT!** Always have a 1-2 man team there to assist you with setting up and breaking down your event.

- **DON'T FREAK OUT!** Planning an event can become very stressful and sometimes chaotic. Don't allow yourself to freak out if things don't go quite like you hoped for. Remember the why.

- **DOCUMENTATION IS KEY!** Always have a sign in sheet to keep record of your volunteer. This can help you for future events.

- **GIVE A GIFT!** Have a few gifts $5.00 gift cards on hand.

- **ACTIONS SPEAK VOLUMES!** From the person with the biggest job to the person with the smallest. Let them know their appreciated.

- GET CREATIVE! Don't be afraid to think outside the box.

- BE A BLESSING! Keep a small food kit in your car.

- GIVE! Donate to other organizations your finances, time, and/or donate your used or new items.

- HAVE RESOURCES AVAILABLE! Direct homeless people to other resources that can help such as a list of shelters, food banks, and places they can shower.

- BE A RESOURCE! Create jobs if you're in the position to.

- BE CONSIDERATE! Don't give the homeless spicy or hot foods. With the low age in water you don't want them to drink up all their water.

- STAY ORGANIZED! Create a schedule to keep your event flowing smoothly and to ensure that everything is on track.

- **MEASUREMENT!** Monitor progress in at each event.

- **BE STRATEGIC!** Always create a theme for each event.

- **WEATHER REPORTS!** Check the weather before any outside events.

About the Author

Dishambra McQueen, a native of Dallas, TX is a versatile, fearless, ambitious, and vibrant actress, model, motivational speaker, and entrepreneur. Her light shines bright both on stage and in the community.

McQueen is no stranger to the everyday struggles of life. As a child, she was diagnosed with dyslexia. This made things very difficult for her growing up. However, as an adult it has motivated her to work even harder. At the age of 28 she found herself homeless. After a year of sleeping in her truck at Walmart, she made a vow. Once she was able to take care of herself again she would help other people enduring the same hardship. She did just that by forming the "McQueen Foundation".

Her inspirational journey of homelessness allows her to give others hope by sharing her story. While doing this, McQueen also speaks, encourages and inspires both the homeless and those with disabilities.

She lets them know that no matter how difficult the journey, they too can accomplish anything they put their minds to. It's because of those adversities that McQueen refuses to allow any of it to stop her from dreaming big and reaching her goals. She is a firm believer that with a combination of hard work and faith anything is achievable.

McQueen is also a mentor, ordained minister, and massage therapist. She recently launched her newest business venture "Touched By A Queen". Never losing sight of her promise to God, she inspires everywhere she goes and strives daily to impact the lives of others, no matter what she's doing. She is a true example that no matter how high the odds are stacked against you, you can achieve anything your heart desires.

Resources

The list below are some locations that provide services for the homeless in Dallas and Tarrant County. Contact the locations directly for more information. Please research all other locations.

Saturday Meal Providers:

Mercy House
1100 W Griffin St
Dallas, TX 75215
(214) 663-6782
9:00 a.m. - 2:00 p.m.

Solomon's Porch Hands and Hearts Ministries
(214) 827-3927
8:00 a.m. - 2:00 p.m.

St. Paul's Body and Soul
1816 Routh St.
Dallas, TX 75201
(214) 922-0000
8:00 a.m. and Sunday at 3:30 p.m.

Medical Care:

AIDS Interfaith Network
2707 N. Stemmons FWY, Suite 120
Dallas, TX 75207
(214) 943-4444

Agape Clinic
4105 Junius St.
Dallas, TX 75246
(214) 824-2533

Baylor Hospital
3501 Junius St.
Dallas, TX 75246
(214) 820-0111

LifeNet
9708 Skillman St.
Dallas, TX 75235
(214) 221-5433

Solace Counseling
1475 Prudential Dr.
Dallas, TX 75235
(214) 522-4640

Thrive Women's Clinic Central Dallas
6500 Greenville Ave Suite 405
Dallas, Tx 75206
(214) 369-6281

Thrive Women's Clinic East Dallas
12959 Jupiter Rd. Suite 260
Dallas, TX 75238
(214) 343-9263

Thrive Women's Clinic West Dallas
3901 Holystone Rd.

Dallas, TX 75212
(214) 905-9068

Substance Abuse:

Dallas Behavioral Healthcare
800 Kirnwood Dr.
Desoto, TX 75115
(972) 982-0900

Turtle Creek
2707 Routh St.
Dallas, TX 75201
(214) 871-2483

Pay to Stay:

Adult Rehabilitation Ministries
1128 Reverend CBT St.
Dallas, TX 75203
214-943-5010
Pay-to-stay $10.00 a day

Dallas Life
1100 Cadiz St.
Dallas, TX 75215
(214) 421-1380
Pay-to-stay $10.00 a day

Clothing & Hygiene:

Cornerstone Clothing Closet
2713 S. Ervay St.

Dallas, TX 75215
(214) 426-5468
Provides showers on Tuesdays at 6:00 p.m. and clothing and showers Thursdays and Saturdays at 11:00 a.m.

Crossroads Community Services
1822 Young St.
Dallas, TX 75201
(972) 560-2511
Provides clothing and food.

Transitional Housing/Services:

Presbyterian Night Shelter in Fort Worth
2400 Cypress St
Fort Worth, TX 76102
(817) 632-7400

Tarrant County Samaritan House
929 Hemphill St
Fort Worth, TX 76104
(817) 332-6410

Interfaith Housing Coalition
5612 Ross Ave.
Dallas, TX 75206
(214) 827-7220

Reconciliation Outreach
1421 N. Peak
Dallas, TX 75204
(214) 545-6500
Provides affordable housing and year long discipline

and recovery services.

Alliance (214) 670-1100

VA Homeless Locations:

VA Medical Center, Homeless Programs
4500 S. Lancaster Rd. Bldg. 71A
Dallas, TX
Monday – Friday 8:00 a.m. – 3:00 p.m.

Veteran's Resource Center
4900 S. Lancaster Rd.
Dallas, TX
Tuesday – Friday 7:00 a.m. – 4:00 p.m.

Shelters:
Austin Street
2929 Hickory St.
Dallas, TX 75226
(214) 428-4242

The Bridge
1818 Cosicana St.
Dallas, TX 75201
(214) 670-1101

Center of Hope (Union Gospel Mission)
4815 Cass St.
Dallas, TX 75235
(214) 638-2988

Family Gateway
711 S. Saint Paul St.
Dallas, TX 75201
(214) 823-4500

Union Gospel Mission (Men Only)
3211 Irving Blvd.
Dallas, TX 75247
(214) 637- 6117

Other:

Genesis Women's Shelter
(214) 946-4357
Provides 24-hour emergency shelter, transitional housing, and trauma recovery.

Restored Hope Ministries (469) 334-0035
Provides recovery for women affected by sex trafficking.

CitySquare
1600 S. Malcolm X Blvd.
Dallas, TX 75226
(214) 828-2696
Provides food pantry access, housing, neighborhood support services, and job training.

The Stewpot
1835 Young St.
Dallas, TX 75217
(214) 746-2785
Provides clothing and hygiene, dental services, mail distribution, medical assistance, mental health services,

has case workers, payee assistance Monday – Friday 8:00 a.m. – 11:45 a.m. and 1:00 p.m. – 3:45 p.m. (Tuesdays at 2:45 p.m.)

VA Homeless Housing Info Line
1-800-849-3597 ext. 78955

Veteran Crisis Hotline
1-800-273-8255

VA National Call Center for Homeless Veteran Resources 1-877-424-3838

Glossary

Volunteer: A person who freely offers to take part in an enterprise or undertake a task.

Homeless: A person without a home, and therefore typically living on the streets.

Charity: An organization set up to provide help and raise money for those in need.

Organization: A body of people with a particular purpose.

Fundraiser: A person whose job or task is to seek financial support for a charity **501c(3):** IRS Federal Tax-Exemption Status-501(c)(3) Organizations. Most PTAs are classified as tax-exempt **501(c)(3)** Public Charities under the Internal Revenue Code (IRC). ... They must not violate certain restrictions that apply to their **501(c)(3)** classification.

Shelter: A place giving temporary protection from bad weather or danger

Veteran: Any person who served honorably on active duty in the armed forces of the United States. Discharges marked "general and under honorable conditions. They would be considered a veteran no matter how long they served.

Nonprofit Marketing: Is activities and strategies that spread the message of the organization.

Donations: Something that is given to an organization to help its cause.

Partnering: Establishing a long-term relationship based on mutual trust and teamwork

Homeless Community: A group of individuals living in the same place and having a particular characteristic in common.

Dishambra McQueen

www.ingramcontent.com/pod-product-compliance
Lightning Source LLC
Chambersburg PA
CBHW071912070526
44583CB00016B/1950